Spanish Phrasebook

1,001 Easy to Learn Spanish Phrases

Jose Alvarez

Table of Contents

Introduction – Introducción

If you're reading this phrase book, good job. Learning Spanish is an incredible investment no matter what the reason. Spanish is one of the top five most spoken languages in the world and many Spanish-speaking countries are incredible places to visit, hosting some of the world's most beautiful attractions. Heck, four continents have countries where Spanish is an official language!

Perhaps you're going on vacation to Peru to climb Machu Picchu or have a client from Madrid, being able to communicate in the local language will go along way in enhancing your experiences and strengthen relationships.

As an English speaker can you learn Spanish quickly and easily? It is definitely possible. Thankfully there are many similarities between the two languages, although many differences exist as well. However with the prevalence of the Spanish language, by combining this book with other sources such as media, TV, movies, and music you can fluidly navigate your way and be chatting up the locals in no time.

Differences Between English & Spanish
– Las Diferencias Entre Inglés y Español

Masculine and feminine forms

Possibly the biggest difference between English and Spanish is that in Spanish, many words have a masculine and feminine form. Many nouns and adjectives change depending on whether it is refers to a male or female. You can tell if it is masculine or feminine depending on the last letter of the word. There are various masculine endings but words that end in the letter "o" are always masculine, and therefore the article that precedes the word will be "el," although there are few exceptions. For example the word "hermano" will use el, "el hermano."

For feminine words, the last letter would be, "a" and the feminine article would be "la." Example: "la hermana," the sister. Also it is worth noting that words that end with the suffix, "-ción" are almost always feminine as well. And example would be, "la habitación."

For many adjectives the word's gender is interchangeable, changing depending on if the adjective is referring to a male or female subject. For example, to say the man is good-looking in Spanish, you would say, "El hombre es guapo." When referring to a female you would change the "o" at the end of guapo to an "a," "La mujer es guapa."

Accents

Visually, you can tell the difference between Spanish and English just by reading the two. Whereas in English we must learn to instinctively tell which syllables to emphasize, the Spanish language made it a little bit easier by placing an accent mark (´) above the letter that needs to be stressed. One rule to keep in mind is that only vowels will be stressed and marked with the symbol. For example, "la dirección," or "qué."

Punctuation

Another visual difference between English and Spanish is punctuation. While commas and periods are uniform in the two languages, exclamation points and question marks are not. For sentences and phrases meant to be questions start with an upside down question mark (¿) and end with the normal question mark we always see at the end of a sentence. Sentences and phrases meant to portray excitement and end with exclamation points (!) start with an upside down exclamation point (¡) and end with one as well. Examples: ¿Dónde estás? ¡Vamos!

Pronunciation

It is essential that you learn the Spanish alphabet and the sound each letter makes. Unlike English, Spanish words are pronounced exactly as they are written. And although that may sound easy enough, you don't want to make a food of yourself by butchering the pronunciation of simple words when speaking to a local.

Grammar

In both Spanish and English sentences are formed in the same manner. Subject + Verb + Object. Although in Spanish there is a bit more flexibility, generally the words that necessitate more emphasis in a given phrase will come last.

One key part of Spanish is that the subject is often not needed in a phrase. If the verb is conjugated, then the subject is not needed. For example instead of writing, "él va a casa" (he goes home) you can write, "va a casa." And the meaning is the same.

Object pronouns

Unlike English, the Spanish language allows the attachment object pronouns to the ends of words. Though they can only be attached to three verb forms: the infinitive, gerund, and affirmative commands. The pronoun is written as if it were apart of the verb. Example: Voy a despedirte. I am going to say good-bye to you.

Basic Spanish Lessons – Lecciónes Básicas de Español

Verb conjugation

Spanish has a uniform conjugation method for specific infinitive verb endings. Verbs ending in –ar all have the same conjugations apart from a few irregular verbs, and the same goes for verbs ending in –er/ir. Like English, the verbs are conjugated depending on the subject.

Verb conjugations for each subject

Verbs ending in –ar

Yo (me): -o

Tú (you): -as

Él/Ella/Usted (Him, Her, You – formal): -a

Ellos/Ellas/Ustedes (Them masculine and feminine, you all formal): -an

Vosotros (you all): -áis

Nosotros (us, we): - amos

Verbs ending in –er/ir

Yo: -o

Tú: -es

Él/Ella/Usted: -e

Ellos/Ellas/Ustedes: -en

Vosotros: -ís

Nosotros: amos

European Spanish vs. Latin American Spanish

Although each country in the Spanish-speaking world has their own distinctive characteristics, there are stark differences between the Spanish spoken in Spain and that spoken throughout Latin America.

First is the vocabulary, as many words have different meanings. For example the word "carro" in Latin America is used for *car* while in Spain, carro means *cart*. While there are countless words with double meanings, there is one that is especially worth pointing out, the word "coger." In Spain coger means, to collect or to get. While in many Latin American countries the word means *to fuck*. So be careful if you say you're going to, "coger alguien" in Latin America.

Second, and probably the most obvious contrast is pronunciation of the letters "c" and "z." In Spain the letters are pronounced like *th* in English, while throughout Latin America they are pronounced more or less like an *s*. Therefore the word "cerca" in Spain is pronounced *th – ehr – ka*. While in Latin America it would be *ser – ka*.

Third, in Spain they commonly use vosotros as a subject pronouns, rarely using usedes or even usted. Of course usted is a more formal way of addressing someone as "you." In Latin America, it is the opposite. They rarely use vosotros, instead using ustedes and often use usted instead of tú.

Object Pronouns

Me → me

Te → you

Le → him/her, you (formal)

Les → them, you all (formal)

Os → you all

Nos → us

These are used with reflexive verbs.

B and V

In much of the Spanish-speaking world the letters B and V are pronounced the same. At the beginning of a word, or if they follow an M or N the letters are pronounced like B in the word "box." Otherwise they take on a soft B sound.

LL

In general, the LL letter combination takes on the Y sound like in "yellow." However in Argentina and Uruguay, it is pronounced like the letter S.

Prefixes and Their Meanings

Ante - previously, behorehand

Anti – opposition

Auto - self, to do it oneself

Contra – opposition

Con - addition or association

De - downward, separation, origin, emphasis, opposite of root word meaning

En – inside, connecting, enclosing

Ex - outside of, further

Extra - over, outside of, exceed

In - inside

Inter - between, among

Para - with, to the side of, against

Per – intensity, could signify "bad"

Pre - prior to, priority, before

Pro – instead of, before, go forward, in favor of

Re – repetition, move back, oppose

Sub – below, inferior

Uni – solitary, alone

Numbers - Numeros

One

Uno

(oo – no)

Two

Dos

(doe – ss)

Three

Trés

(trey – ss)

Four

Cuatro

(kwa – tro)

Five

Cinco

(sin – ko)

Six

Seis

(say   ss)

Seven

Siete

(see – eh –te)

Eight

Ocho

(oh – cho)

Nine

Nueve

(nu – eh – vey)

Ten

Diez

(dee – ace)

Eleven

Once

(wwn – sey)

Twelve

Doss

(doe – sey)

Thirteen

Trece

(trey – sey)

Fourteen

Catorce

(kah – tor – sey)

Fifteen

Quince

(keen – sey)

Sixteen

Dieciseis

(dee – ace – ee – seys)

Seventeen

Diecisiete

(dee – ace – ee –see – ey – te)

Eighteen

Dieciocho

(dee – ace – ee – oh – cho)

Nineteen

Diecinueve

(dee - ace – ee – nu – eh – ve)

Twenty

Viente

(ven – te)

Thirty

Trienta

(Tre – en – ta)

Forty

Cuarenta

(quar – en – ta)

Fifty

Cincuenta

(sin – quen – ta)

Sixty

Seisenta

(sey – sen – ta)

Seventy

Setenta

(sey – ten – ta)

Eighty

Ochenta

(oh – chen – ta)

Ninety

Noventa

(no – ven – ta)

One hundred

Cien

(see – en)

Two hundred

Doscientos

(dohs – see – ehn – tohs)

Five Hundred

Quinientos

(keen – yen – tohs)

One thousand

Mil

(meel)

Five thousand

Cinco mil

(seen – ko meel)

One million

Un million

(oon mee – yohn)

Ten million

Diez milliones

(dee – ehs mee – yohn – es)

One billion

Mil milliones

(meel mee – yohn – es)

One trillion

Un billon

(oon bee – yohn)

How many do you have?

¿Cuántos tienes?

(*kwan* – tos tee – en – ehs)

Various

Varios

(vahr – ee – ohs)

Lots/A lot

Mucho

(moo – cho)

More

Más

(*mahs*)

Less

Menos

(meh – nos)

Time and Date – Día y Fecha

What is the date?

¿Cual es la fecha?

(qual es la fe – cha)

What day is today?

¿Qué día es hoy?

(ke dee – a es oi)

Monday

Lunes

(loo – nes)

Tuesday

Martes

(mar – tes)

Wednesday

Miercoles

(me – air – ko – les)

Thursday

Jueves

(who – eh – ves)

Friday

Viernes

(vee – air – nes)

Saturday

Sábado

(sah – bah – doh)

Sunday

Domingo

(doe – ming – go)

January

Enero

(en – ehr – oh)

February

Febrero

(feb – rer – oh)

March

Marzo

(mar – so)

April

Abril

(ah – breel)

May

Mayo

(mah – yo)

June

Junio

(hoon – eeo)

July

Iulio

(hoo – leeo

August

Agosto

(ah – gos – toh)

September

Septiembre

(sep – tee – em – bre)

October

Octubre

(ok – too – bre)

November

Noviembre

(no – vee – em – bre)

December

Diciembre

(dee – cee – em – bre)

Next weekend

El finde que viene

(el feen – de ke vee – en – eh)

The following weekend

El finde siguiente

(el feen – de ke vee – en – eh)

Next week

La semana que viene

(la se – mah – nah ke vee – en – eh)

The following week

La semana siguiente

(la se – mah – nah ke vee – en – eh)

During the week

Entre semana

(en – trey se – ma – na)

Weekend

Fin de semana

(feen de se – ma – na)

What time is it?

¿Qué hora es?

(ke o - ra es)

It is three thirty

Son las tres y media

(sohn las trey - s ee mey – dee – ah)

One hour

Una hora

(oo – na o – ra)

Half hour

Media hora

(mey – dee – ah or – ah)

What time?

¿A qué hora?

(ah ke o ra)

When

Cuándo

(*kwan* – doh)

Season

Estación

(es – ta – see – *ohn*)

Fall

Otoño

(oh – ton – *yo)*

Winter

Invierno

(een – vee – ehr – no)

Spring

Primavera

(pree – mah – ver – ah)

Summer

Verano

(ver – ah – no)

Morning

Mañana

(ma – nya – na)

Afternoon

Tarde

(tar – day)

Day

Día

(*dee* – ah)

Night/Evening

Noche

(no – chey)

Last night

Anoche

(ah – no – che)

Dawn

Madrugada

(ma – dru – ga – da)

Dusk

Anochecer

(a – no – che – ser)

Early

Temprano

(tem – para – no)

Soon

Pronto

(pron – toe)

Before

Antes

(an – tes)

Late

Tarde

(tar – dey)

Later

Luego

(loo – eh – go)

In the morning

Por la mañana

(pour la man – *ya* na)

In the afternoon

Por la tarde

(pour la tar – de)

In the evening

Por la noche

(pour la no – che)

Since what time?

¿Desde qué hora?

(des – de *ke* oh – ra)

Since when?

¿Desde cuándo?

(des – de *kwan* – doh)

Since three

Desde las tres

(des – de lahs treys)

One hour ago

Hace una hora

(ah – se oona oh – ra)

A second

Un segundo

(oon seh – goon – doh)

A minute

Un minuto

(oon meen – oo – toh)

Noon

Mediodía

(meh – dee – oh – *dee* ah)

Midnight

Medionoche

(meh – dee – oh – no – che)

Family - Familia

We're family

Somos familia

(so – mohs fah – meel – ee – ah)

Father

Padre

(pa – dre)

Dad

Papa

(pa – pa)

Mother

Madre

(ma – dre)

Mom

Mama

(ma – ma)

Brother

Hermano

(ehr – ma – no)

Sister

Hermana

(ehr – ma – na)

Siblings

Hermanos

(ehr – ma – nos)

We're siblings

Somos hermanos

(so – mohs ehr – mahn – ohs)

Cousin

Primo/Prima

(pree – mo/pree – ma)

We're cousins

Somos primos

(so – mohs pree – mohs)

Uncle

Tío

(*tee* – o)

Aunt

Tía

(*tee* – a)

Grandfather

Abuelo

(a – bwey – lo)

Grandmother

Abuela

(a – bwey – la)

Great Grandfather

Bisabuelo

(bees – a – bwey – lo)

Great Grandmother

Bisabuela

(bees – a –bwey – la)

In-laws

Los suegros

(low – s swe – gros)

Father-in-law

Suegro

(swey – gro)

Mother-in-law

Suegra

(swey – gro)

Brother-in-law

Cuñado

(koo – *nya* – do)

Sister-in-law

Cuñada

(koo – *nya* – da)

Son-in-law

Yerno

(yehr – no)

Daughter-in-law

Nuora

(nwehr – ah)

Stepfather

Padrastro

(pa – dras – tro)

Stepmother

Madrastra

(ma – dras – tra)

Stepbrother

Hermanastro

(ehr – mahn – as – tro)

Stepsister

Hermanastra

(ehr – mahn – as – tra)

Son

Hijo

(ee – ho)

Daughter

Hija

(ee – ha)

Grandson

Nieto

(nee – ye – to)

Granddaughter

Nieta

(nee – ye – ta)

Stepson

Hijastro

(ee – has – tro)

Stepdaughter

Hijastra

(ee – has – tra)

Nephew

Sobrino

(so – bree – no)

Niece

Sobrina

(so – bree – na)

Boyfriend

Novio

(no – vee – o)

Girlfriend

Novia

(no – vee – a)

Child

Niño/Niña

(ni – *nyo*/ni – *nya*)

Identical twin brother

Gemelo

(he – meh – lo)

Identical twin sister

Gemela

(he – meh – la)

Twin brother

Mellizo

(meh – yee – so)

Twin sister

Melliza

(meh – yee – sa)

Godfather

Padrino

(pa – dree – no)

Godmother

Madrina

(ma – dree – na)

Husband

Marido

(ma – ree – do)

Wife

Mujer

(moo – hair)

Relatives

Familiares

(fa – meel – ee – ar – es)

How many siblings do you have?

¿Cuántos hermanos tienes?

(*quan* – tos ehr – mah – nos tee – ye – nes)

Directions – Direcciónes

Where

Dónde

(*dohn* – dey)

Where is it?

¿Dónde está?

(*dohn* – dey es – *tah*)

Where is the hotel?

¿Dónde está el hotel?

(*dohn* – dey es – *tah* el oh – tell)

Where is the subway?

¿Dónde está el metro?

(*dohn* – dey es – *tah* el meh – tro)

Where is the bus?

¿Por dónde pasa el autobús?

(pour *dohn* – dey pah – sah el ahou – toh *–boos)*

Where are the taxis?

¿Dónde están los taxis?

(*dohn* – dey es – *tahn* los tax – ees)

What is the address?

¿Cuál es la dirección?

(*kwal* es la dee – reck – see – *ohn*)

How do I get to...

Como llego a...

(ko – mo ye – go ah)

Do you have a map?

¿Tienes un mapa?

(tee – ye – nes oon mah – pah)

Is it near?

¿Está cerca?

(es – *tah* ser – ka)

Is it far?

¿Está lejos?

(es – *tah* ley – hos)

Go back

Vuelva

(vu – el – va)

Follow

Seguir

(sey – geer)

Cross

Cruzar

(kru – sar)

Toward

Hacía

(ah – *see* – ah)

Straight

Recto

(reck   toh)

Left

Izquierda

(ees – kee – air – da)

Right

Derecha

(deh – reh – cha)

Near

Cerca

(ser – ka)

Far

Lejos

(ley – hos)

Go up

Subir

(su – beer)

Go down

Bajar

(ba – har)

Up

Arriba

(ah – ree – ba)

Down

Abajo

(ah – ba – ho)

Behind

Detrás de

(dey – trahs dey)

In front of

Enfrente de

(en – fren – te dey)

Go straight

Sigue recto

(see – gey reck – toh)

Go that way

Vaya en aquella dirección

(va – yah en ah – ke – ya dee – reck – *seeohn*)

Turn right

Gira a la derecha

(hee – rah ah la dey – reh – cha)

Turn left

Gira a la izquierda

(hee – rah a la ees – kee – yer – dah)

Drop me off here, please

Déjame aquí por favor

(*dey* – ha – meh ah – *kee* pour fah – vour)

To walk

Caminar

(kah – mee – nar)

To walk

Andar

(ahn – dar)

To drive

Conducir

(kohn – du – seer)

Street

La calle

(lah ka – ye)

Highway

La carretera

(lah kar – re – te – ra)

Roundabout

La rotonda

(lah roh – tohn – dah)

Corner

La esquina

(lah es – kee – nah)

The next Street

La calle siguiente

(lah ka – ye see – gi – en – te)

Greetings – Saludos

Hello

Hola

(oh – lah)

Good morning

Buenos días

(bwey – nos *dee* – as)

Good afternoon

Buenas tardes

(bwey – nas tar – deys)

Good evening

Buenas noches

(bwey – nas no – ches)

How are you?

¿Como estás?

(koh – moh es – *tas*)

Fine

Bien

(bee – en)

Very well

Muy bien

(moo – ee bee – en)

So-so

Más o menos

(*mahs* oh meh – nos)

How's it going?

¿Cómo te va?

(koh – moh te vah)

How is everything?

¿Qué tal?

(*keh* tal)

What's your name?

¿Cómo te llamas?

(*koh* – moh te ya – mahs)

What is his/her name?

¿Cómo se llama?

(*ko* – mo se ya – ma)

My name is...

Me llamo...

(meh ya – moh)

I'm David

Soy David

(soy dah – veed)

Nice to meet you

Mucho gusto

(moo – choh goos – toh)

Pleasure to meet you

Un placer

(oon pla – ser)

Goodbye

Adiós

(ah –dee – *os*)

Have a good day

Ten un buen día

(ten oon bweyn *dee* –ah)

See you son

Hasta pronto

(ahs – tah pron – toh)

See you later

Hasta luego

(ahs – tah loo – eh – go)

See you tomorrow

Hasta mañana

(ahs – tah mahn - *ya* – nah)

Goodnight

Buenas noches

(bwey – nahs noh – ches)

Where do you live?

¿Dónde vives?

(*dohn* – deh vee – ves)

I live in...

Vivo en...

(vee – vo ehn)

Where are you from?

¿De dónde eres?

(dey *dohn* – dey eh – res)

I am from the United States

Soy de los Estados Unidos

(soy dey los es – tah – dohs oo – nee – dohs)

This is my friend

Éste es mi amigo/amiga

(es – te es *mee* ah – mee – go/ah – mee - gah)

Come with me

Ven conmigo

(ven con – mee – go)

I had a wonderful time

Lo pasé muy bien

(low pah – *sey* mooy bee – en)

Jobs & Education – Trabajos y Educación

To work

Trabajar

(trah – bah – har)

I have to go to work

Tengo que irme a trabajar

(ten – go ke eer – meh ah trah- bah – har)

What do you do?

¿A que te dedicas?

(ah ke te deh – dee – kas)

I work for...

Trabajo por...

(trah – bah –ho pour)

Where do you work?

¿Dónde trabajas?

(dohn – dey trah – bah – hahs)

I work in advertising

Trabajo en publicidad

(trah – bah – ho en poob – lee – see – dahd)

Career

Carrera

(ka – rehr – ah)

Office

La oficina

(lah oh – fee – see – nah)

Firm

El bufete

(el bu – fe – te)

Office park

El parque empresarial

(el par – ke em – preh – sah – reeal)

Co-worker

Compañero

(kom – pahn – *ye* – ro)

Colleague

Colega

(koh – leh – gah)

Business partner

Socio

(so – see – oh)

Company

La compañía

(lah kom – pahn – *ee* – ah)

Enterprise

Empresa

(em – preh – sa)

Business

Negocio

(neh – go –see – oh)

Agreement

Acuerdo

(ah – kwer – doh)

Contract

Contrato

(kon – tra – toh)

To hire

Contratar

(kon – tra – tar)

They hired me

Me cogieron

(meh ko – hee – ehr – ohn)

Interview

Entrevista

(en – trey – vees – tah)

Employee

Empleado

(em – play – adoh)

Boss

Jefe

(heh – fe)

Executive

Ejecutivo

(eh – heh – koo – teevo)

Employment

Empleo

(em – pley – o)

Staff

Personal

(pehr – sohn – al)

Job offer

Oferta de empleo

(oh – fehr – ta de em – ple – o)

Training

Formación

(for – mah – see – *ohn*)

Engineer

Ingeniero

(een – hen – yero)

Scientist

Científico

(see – en – teef – ee – koh)

Doctor (medical)

Médico

(*meh* – dee – koh)

Schedule a doctor visit

Programar una cita con el medico

(pro – grahm – ar oona see – ta kon el *meh* – dee – ko)

Lawyer

Abogado

(ah – boh – gah – doh)

Police officer

Policía

(poh – lee – *see* – ah)

Teacher

Profesor

(pro – fes – or)

Journalist

Periodista

(pear – ee –oh – dees – tah)

Intern

Becario

(beh – car – eeoh)

Businessman

Hombre de negocios

(ohm – brey dey ne – go – see – ohs)

Entrepreneur

Emprendedor

(em – pren – dey – dor)

Owner

Propietario

(pro – pee – eh – tar – eeo)

Freelance

Autónomo

(ow – toh – no – moh)

Study

Estudiar

(es – tu – dee – are)

University

Universidad

(oo – nee – vehr – see – dahd)

Primary school

Colegio

(koh – ley – he – oh)

High school

Instituto

(een – stee – to – toh)

Subject

Asignatura

(ah – sig – nah – tour – ah)

Faculty

Facultad

(fa – cool – tahd)

Degree

Carrera

(car – rer – ah)

Studies

Estudios

(es – too – dee – os)

Class

Clase

(kla – sey)

Exam

Examen

(ex – ahm – en)

Grade

Nota

(no – tah)

What do you study?

¿Qué estudias?

(ke es – too – dee – ahs)

What did you study?

¿Qué estudiaste?

(ke es – too – dee – as – te)

I study at the university

Estudio en la universidad

(es – too – dee – oh en lah ooni – ver – see – dahd)

I am studying biology

Estoy estudiando biológico

(es – toy es – too – dee – andoh bee – oh loh hc ko)

Postgraduate degree

Postgrado

(post – grah – doh)

Master's degree

Un master

(oon mas – tehr)

I am getting a master's degree in education

Estoy estudiano un master de educación

(es – toy es- too – dee – ando oon mas – tehr dey ed – oo – ka –*seeohn*)

Course

Curso

(koor – so)

I am taking a business course

Estoy en un curso de negocios

(es – toy en oon koor – so dey neh – go – seeohs)

We are studying hard

Estamos estudiando muy fuerte

(es – tah – mos es – too – dee – ando mooy fwer – tey)

Semester

Semestre

(seh – mes – trey)

Lesson

Lección

(lek – see – *ohn*)

Student

Estudiante

(es – too – dee – ahn – te)

Doctorate

Doctorado

(dok tor ado)

Thesis

Tesis

(te – sees)

I get good grades

Yo saco buenas notas

(yo sa – ko bwey – nahs no – tahs)

Classmate

Compañero de clase

(kom – pan – *ye* – ro dey kla – sey)

Homework

Tarea

(tar – ey – ah)

Pen

Bolígrafo

(bo – *lee* grah – fo)

Pencil

Lápiz

(*la* – pees)

Eraser

Goma

(go – ma)

Paper

Papel

(pa – pehl)

Notebook

Cuaderno

(kwa – dehr – no)

Book

Libro

(lee – bro)

Folder

Carpeta

(kar – peh – ta)

Backpack

Mochila

(mo – chee – la)

Board

Pizarra

(pee – sar – ra)

Chalk

Tiza

(tee – sa)

Hotels & Lodging – Hoteles y Alojamiento

Hotel

Hotel

(oh – tel)

Guest

Huésped

(*weys* – ped)

Hostel

Hostal

(ohs – tal)

Youth hostel

Albergue juvenil

(al – behr – gey hu – ven – eel)

Room

Habitación

(ahbee – tah – see – *ohn*)

Reservation

Reservación

(re – ser – vah – see – *ohn*)

Check in

Registrarse

(re – hees – trar – sey)

Bed

Cama

(kah – mah)

Boarding house

Pensión

(pen – see – *ohn)*

Double room

Habitación doble

(ab – ee – tah – see – *ohn* doh – bley)

Key

Llave

(ya – ve)

Do you have the keys?

¿Tienes las llaves?

(tee – en – es las ya – vehs)

Elevator

Ascensor

(ass – sen – sor)

Double bed

Cama doble

(doh – bley ka – ma)

King-size bed

Cama matrimonio

(ka – ma ma – tree – moneeo)

Lobby

Vestíbulo

(ves – *tee* - bu – lo)

Room service

Servicio de habitación

(ser – vee – see – o de ah – bee – tah – cee – *ohn*)

How much per night?

¿Cuánto cobra por noche?

(kwan – to co – bra pour no – che)

Is there anything cheaper?

¿Hay algo más barato?

(ay al – go *mas* ba – ra – toh)

Hi, I wanted to reserve a room for this weekend

Hola, quería reservar una habitación para este fin de semana

(oh – la ker – *eeah* re – ser – var oonah ahb – eetah – seeohn es – te feen de se – mah – nah)

For how many people?

¿Para cuántas personas?

(pa – ra *kwan* – tahs per – sohn – as)

Is there Wifi in the room?

¿Hay wifi en la habitación?

(ay wee – fee en la ahb – eetah – see - *ohn*)

Concierge

Conserje

(kon – ser – hey)

Five-star

Cinco estrellas

(sin – ko es – trey – yas)

Gym

Gimnasio

(him – nas – eeoh)

Pool

Piscina

(pees – see – nah)

I have a reservation

Tengo una reserva

(ten – go oonah re – ser – va)

Rooftop terrace

Azotea

(ah – so – tay – ah)

Beach

Playa

(plai – ah)

How far is the hotel from the beach?

¿A qué distancia se encuentra el hotel de la playa?

(ah *ke* dees – tan – seeah se en – kwen – tra el oh – tel de la plai – ah)

Extra bed

Cama supletoria

(kah – ma soo – ple – tor – eeah)

Bathtub

Bañera

(bahn – *yera*)

Hairdryer

El secador de pelo

(el se – ka – dohr de peh – lo)

Hanger

Percha

(pehr – cha)

Sink

Lavabo

(lah – va – bo)

Window

Ventana

(ven – tahn – nah)

Pillow

Almohada

(al – mo – ah – da)

Lamp

Lámpara

(lam – par – ah)

Safe (lockbox)

Caja fuerte

(ka – ha fwer – te)

Shower

Ducha

(du – cha)

Shampoo

Champú

(cham – poo)

Television

Televisión

(te – le vees – ee – *ohn*)

Toilet

Inordoro

(een – or – doh – ro)

Sheets

Sábanas

(*sah* – bah – nahs)

Towel

Toalla

(toh – ay – ya)

Water

Agua

(ah – gwa)

I'll be staying three nights

Me voy a quedar tres noches

(meh voy ah ke – dar trehs no – ches)

Please give me a wake-up call at 8 a.m.

Por favor, llame para despertarme a las ocho de la mañana

(pour fah – vour ya – me pa – ra des – pehr – tar – meh ah las oh – cho de la mahn – *ya* na)

Our room hasn't been cleaned

No han limpiado nuestro cuarto

(no ahn leem – pee – ah – doh nwes – tro cwar – toh)

Are there any rooms available?

¿Hay habitaciones disponibles?

(ay ahb – ee – tah – see – ohnes dees – pon – ee – bles)

Sorry, we're full

Lo siento, estamos completos

(low see – en – toh es – ta – mos cohm – ple – tos)

Suite

Suite

(sw – eet)

Air conditioning

Aire acondicionado

(ay – rey ah – kon – dee – seeoh – nado)

Check out is at 11:00 am

A las 11 de la mañana debe dejar la habitación

(ah las ohn – se de la ma – *nya* – na de – bey de – har la ahb – ee – tah – see – *ohn*)

Boarding house

Pensión

(pen – see – *ohn*)

Full board

Pensión completa

(pen – see – *ohn* kom – ple – ta)

Half board

Media pensión

(meh – dee – ah pen – see – *ohn*)

I would like…

Me gustaría…

(meh goos – tar – *eeah*)

I'd like a room with a view

Me gustaría una habitación con vistas

(meh goos – tar – *eeah* oonah ahb – ee – ta – see –*ohn* kon vees – tahs)

Balcony

Balcón

(bahl – *kon*)

I'd like a room with a balcony

Me gustaría una habitación con balcón

(meh goos – tar – *eeah* oonah ahb – ee – ta – see – *ohn* kon bahl – *kon*)

Porter

Portero

(pour – tear – oh)

Bellhop

Botones

(boh – ton – es)

Manager

Gerente

(he – ren – te)

I'd like to speak with the manager

Me gustaría hablar con el gerente

(meh goos – tar – *eeah* kon el he – ren – te)

Bill

La cuenta

(la kwen – ta)

Receipt

Factura

(faq – toor – ah)

Feelings – Sentimientos

To be

Estar

(es – tar)

I am…

Estoy…

(es – toy)

Sad

Triste

(trees – te)

Happy

Feliz

(fel – ees)

Unhappy

Infeliz

(een – fel – eez)

Angry

Enfadado

(en – fah – dah – doh)

Confused

Confundido

(kon – fun – dee – doh)

In love

Enamorado

(en –ah – mor – ado)

Stressed

Estresado

(es – tres – ado)

Overwhelmed

Agobiado

(ah – go – bee – ado)

Strong

Fuerte

(fwer – te)

Weak

Debíl

(de – *beel*)

Hurt

Dolido

(doh – lee - doh)

Does it hurt?

¿Te duele?

(te dwel – eh)

Exciting

Ilusionante

(ee – lu – sioh – nante)

Boring

Aburrido

(ah – bur – ree – doh)

Timid

Tímido

(tee – mee – doh)

Tired

Cansado

(kahn – sah – doh)

Frieghtened

Asustado

(ah – sus – tah – doh)

I am scared

Tengo miedo

(ten – go mee – ay – doh)

Jealous

Celoso

(sel – oh – so)

Surprised

Sorprendido

(sor – pren – dee – doh)

Content

Contento

(kohn – ten – toh)

Nervous

Nervioso

(nehr – vee – oso)

Busy

Ocupado

(oh – ku – pa – doh)

Worried

Preocupado

(prey – oh – ku – pa – doh)

Furious

Furioso

(foor – ee – oso)

It's embarassing for me

Me da vergüenza

(meh dah vehr – gwen – sah)

Confident

Confiado

(kohn – fee – ado)

Confidence

Confianza

(kohn – fee – ahn – sa)

Sure

Seguro

(se – goo – roh)

Anxious

Ansioso

(an – see – oso)

Depressed

Deprimido

(de – pree – mee – doh)

Patient

Paciente

(pas – ee – en –te)

Proud

Orgulloso

(or – gu – yo – so)

Relieved

Aliviado

(ah – lee – vee – ado)

Restless

Inquieto

(een – kee – et – oh)

Satisfied

Satisfecho

(sa – tees – fe – cho)

Sensitive

Sensitivo

(sen – see – tee – vo)

Uncomfortable

Incómodo

(een – *ko* – mo – doh)

Comfortable

Cómodo

(ko – mo – doh)

Desperate

Desesperado

(des – es – per – ado)

Frustrated

Frustrado

(froos – tra – doh)

Relaxed

Relajado

(re – la – ha – doh)

Insecure

Inseguro

(een – se – gu – ro)

Delighted

Encantado

(en – kan – ta – doh)

Are you sure?

¿Estás seguro?

(es – tas se – goo – roh)

I don't feel well

No me siento bien

(no meh see – en – toh bee – en)

How are you feeling?

¿Cómo te sientes?

(ko – mo te see – en – tes)

I'm fed up

Esoty harto

(es – toy ar – toh)

Sea sick, nausea

Mareado

(mar – eh – ado)

I'm ill

Estoy enfermo

(es – toy en – fehr – mo)

I don't feel like going out

No me apetece a salir

(no meh ah – pe – te – se ah sa – leer)

Fancy, feel like

Apetecer

(ah – pe – te – ser)

Eating, Drinking, & Nightlife
Comer, Beber, y La Vida Nocturna

Eat out

Comer fuera

(koh – mer fwer – ah)

Restaurant

Restaurante

(res – tau – rahn – te)

Fast food

Comida rápida

(koh – mee – da *ra* – pee – da)

Gastronomy

Gastronomía

(gas – tro – no – *mee* – ah)

Breakfast

Desayuno

(des – ay – oo – no)

Lunch

Comida

(koh – mee – da)

Dinner

Cena

(se – na)

Where is a good restaurant?

¿Me recomienda algún restaurante?

(meh re – ko – mee – en – da al – goon res – tau – ran – te)

Do you know a good place to eat?

¿Sabes de un buen sitio para comer?

(sah – bes de oon see – tee – oh pa – ra ko – mehr)

I would like to make a reservation

Querría hacer una reserva

(kehr – *ree* - ah ah – ser oona re – ser – va)

Table for two

Una mesa para dos

(oona meh – sa pa – ra dohs)

Menu

La carta

(la car – ta)

Appetizers

Primer plato

(pree – mehr pla – toh)

Main course

Plato principal

(pla – toh preen – cee – pal)

Dessert

Postre

(pos – tre)

What would you like to drink?

¿Qué quieras para beber?

(*ke* – kee – ehr – as pa – ra beh – behr)

A glass of water, please

Un vaso de agua, por favor

(oon vas – oh de ah – gwa pour fah – vour)

coffee with milk, latte

Café con leche

(kah – *fe* kon le – che)

Beer

Cerveza

(ser – ve – sa)

Wine

Vino

(vee – no)

Red wine

Vino tinto

(vee – no teen – toh)

White wine

Vino blanco

(vee – no blahn – ko)

Whisky

Whisky

(wis – key)

Vodka

Vodka

(vod – ka)

Rum

Ron

(rohn)

Gin

Ginebra

(hen – eh – bra)

Craft beer

Cerveza artesanal

(scr   vc   sa ar – te – san – al)

Vegetarian

Vegetariano

(ve – heh – tear – ee – ano)

Check, please

La cuenta, por favor

(la kwen – tah pour fa – vour)

Tip

Propina

(pro – pee – nah)

Cheers!

¡Salud!

(sa – lood)

It's delicious!

¡Está riquísimo!

(es – ta ree – *kee* – see – mo)

Enjoy your meal

Buen provecho

(bwen pro – ve – cho)

Plate

Plato

(plah – toh)

To be hungry

Tener hambre

(ten – ehr ahm – bre)

I'm hungry

Tengo hambre

(ten – go ahm – bre)

Eat healthy

Comer sano

(ko – mehr sah – no)

Fork

Tenedor

(te – ne – dor)

Knife

Cuchillo

(ku – chee – yo)

Spoon

Cuchara

(ku – cha – rah)

Napkin

Servilleta

(ser – vee – yet – ah)

Glass

Vaso

(va – so)

Bottle

Botella

(bo – te – ya)

Ice

Hielo

(yay – low)

Salt

Sal

(sal)

Pepper

Pimiento

(pee – mee – en – toh)

Sugar

Azúcar

(ah – su – kar)

Soup

Sopa

(so – pa)

Salad

Ensalada

(en – sa – la –da)

Bread

Pan

(pahn)

Butter

Mantequilla

(mahn – te – kee – ya)

Noodles

Fideos

(fee – de – ohs)

Rice

Arroz

(ar – rohs)

Cheese

Queso

(ke – so)

Vegetables

Verduras

(ver – dur – as)

Asparagus

Espárragos

(es – *pahr* – rah – gohs)

Beans

Frijoles

(free – ho – leys)

Beet

Remolacha

(reh – mo – la – cha)

Broccoli

Brécol

(*breh* – kohl)

Carrot

Zanahoria

(sah – nah – ohr – eeah)

Artichoke

Alcachofa

(al – ka – cho – fa)

Cabbage

Col

(kohl)

Cauliflower

Coliflor

(kohl – ee – flohr)

Tomato

Tomate

(toh – mah – te)

Chickpea

Garbanzo

(gar – bahn – so)

Corn

Maíz

(mah – *ees*)

Cucumber

Pepino

(pep – ee – no)

Potato

Papa/patata

(pa – pa / pa – tah – tah)

Sweet potato

Batata/Boniato

(bah – tah –tah / boh – nee – ah – toh)

Mushroom

Champiñón

(cham – peen – *yohn*)

Pepper

Pimiento

(pee – mee – ehn – toh)

Onion

Cebolla

(seh – boi – ya)

Spinach

Espinaca

(es – pee – nah – ka)

Chicken

Pollo

(poyo)

Beef

Carne

(kar – ne)

Pork

Cerdo

(ser – doh)

Fish

Pescado

(pehs – kah – doh)

Spicy

Picante

(pee – kahn – te)

Sweet

Dulce

(dool – se)

Sour

Amargo

(ah – mar – go)

Ice cream

Helado

(el – ah – doh)

Juice

Zumo

(su – moh)

Pie/Cake

Tarta

(tar – ta)

Fruit

Fruta

(fru – ta)

Apple

Manzana

(mahn – sahn – ah)

Plantain

Plátano

(*plah* – tahn – oh)

Banana

Banana

(bah – nah – nah)

Peach

Melocotón

(mehl – oh – ko – *tohn*)

Blueberry

Arándano

(ah – *rahn* – dah – no)

Cherry

Cereza

(seh – reh – sah)

Grape

Uva

(oo – vah)

Lemon

Limón

(lee – *mohn*)

Lime

Lima

(lee – mah)

Pineapple

Piña

(peen – *ya*)

Orange

Naranja

(nah – rahn – ha)

Watermelon

Sandía

(sahn – *dee* – ah)

Raspberry

Frambuesa

(frahm – bwey – sah)

Strawberry

Fresa

(freh – sah)

Pear

Pera

(reh – rah)

Avocado

Aguacate

(ah – gwah – kah – te)

Alcohol

Alcohol

(al – col)

Drink (alcoholic)

Copa

(ko – pa)

Cocktail

Coctel

(kok – tel)

Pub

Mesón

(meh – *sohn)*

Tavern

Taberna

(ta – behr – na)

Bar

Bar

(bur)

Concert

Concierto

(kon – see – ehr – to)

Nightclub

Discoteca

(dees – ko – tek – a)

Dance

Bailar

(bai – lar)

Let's go have a drink

Vamos a tomar algo

(va – mos a to – mar al – go)

Go out

Salir

(sah – leer)

Go out to party

Salir de fiesta

(sah – leer de fee – es – ta)

Party

Fiesta

(fee – es – ta)

Bar hop

Marcha

(mar – cha)

To go bar hopping

Salir de marcha

(sah – leer de mar – cha)

Do I need a reservation?

¿Necesito una reservación?

(neh – she – see – toh oona reh   ser   va   see *ohn*)

Can I see the menu please?

¿Puedo ver la carta, por favor?

(pwe – doh vehr la kar – ta pour fah – vour)

What do you recommend?

¿Qué recomiendas?

(*ke* reh – ko – mee – en – das)

I'm a vegetarian

Soy vegetariano

(soy veh – he – tar – ee – ano)

I'm a vegan

Soy vegano

(soy veh – gahn – o)

I can't have…

No puedo comer/tomar

(no pwe – doh ko – mehr/toh – mar)

I'm allergic to…

Soy alérgetico a…

(soy al – *ehr* – heh – tee – ko ah)

I'm allergic to nuts/ seafood
Tengo alergia a frutos secos/ marisco
(tehn – go ah – ler – hee – ah ah froo – tos seh – kos/ mah – rees – co)

I'm lactose intolerant

Soy intolerante a la lactosa

(soi een – to – leh – rahn – te ah lah lac – to – sah)

What are today's specials?

¿Cuáles son los platos del día de hoy?

(*kwa* – les sohn los plah – tos del *dee* – ah de oy)

I'd like to try a regional dish

Quisiera probar un plato típico de la región

(kees – ee – ehr – ah pro – bar oon plah- toh *tee* – pee – ko de la re – he – ohn)

Can you bring me the check, please?

Me puedes traer la cuenta, por favor?

(meh pwe – des tra – ehr la kwen – ta pour fah – vour)

I'm on a diet

Estoy a régimen

(es – toy ah reh – he – men)

What is in it?

¿De qué consiste?

(de ke kohm – sees – te)

Hobbies & Sports – Aficiónes y Deportes

What are your hobbies?

¿Cuáles son tus aficiónes?

(*kwal* – es sohn tus ah – fee – see – *ohn* – es)

Free time

Tiempo libre

(tee – em – po lee – bre)

I am a fan of...

Soy un fan de...

(soy oon fan de)

I like...

Me gusta...

(meh goos – ta)

To sing

Cantar

(kan – tar)

To play sports

Jugar deportes

(hu – gar de – por – tes)

To listen to music

Escuchar música

(es - ku - char *moos* – ee – ka)

To ride a bike

Montar en bicicleta

(mohn – tar en bee – see – kle – ta)

To fish

Pescar

(pes – kar)

To swim

Nadar

(na – dar)

To collect stamps

Coleccionar sellos

(ko – lek – see – ohn – ar sey – yos)

To play music

Tocar música

(toh – kar *moos* – ee – ka)

To play an instrument

Tocar un instrumento

(Toh – kar oon een – stru – mehn – toh)

Guitar

Guitarra

(gi – tar – rah)

Drums

Tambor

(tam – bor)

Piano

Piano

(pee – ah – no)

Trumpet

Trompeta

(trom – pe –tah)

To hunt

Cazar

(kah – sar)

To work out

Entrenar

(en – tren – ar)

To run

Correr

(kor – rehr)

To cook

Cocinar

(koh – see – nar)

To sew

Cocer

(koh – ser)

Hiking

Senderismo

(sen – der – ees – mo)

Photography

Fotografía

(fo – toh – gra – *eeah*)

Sailing

La vela

(la veh – la)

Chess

Ajedrez

(ah – heh – dres)

Stadium

Estadio

(es – ta – dee – o)

Court

Cancha

(kahn – cha)

Pitch (Soccer)

Césped

(*Sehs* – ped)

Field

Campo

(kahm – po)

Baseball

Beísbol

(beh – *ees* bol)

Basketball

Baloncesto

(bah – lon – ses – toh)

Football

Fútbol americano

(*foo* – t – bol ah – mehr – ee – cano)

Soccer

Fútbol

(*foo* - t – bol)

Golf

Golf

(gohlf)

Hockey

Hockey

(hockey)

Boxing

Boxeo

(box – eh – o)

Tennis

Tenis

(ten – ees)

Volleyball

Volibol

(vo – lee – bol)

To ski

Esquíar

(es – *kee* - ar)

Snowboard

Snowboard

(snowboard)

Mountain climb

Escalar la montaña

(es – ka – lar la mohn – ta – *nya*)

To go surfing

Hacer surf

(ah – ser surf)

To travel

Viajar

(vee – a – har)

To go on vacation

Ir de vacaciones

(eer de va – kah – see – ohn – es)

Watch a game

Ver un partido

(vehr oon par – tee – doh)

Sports game

Partido

(par – tee – doh)

To read

Leer

(le – ehr)

Read books

Leer libros

(le – ehr lee – bros)

To paint

Pintar

(peen – tar)

To draw

Dibujar

(dee – bu – har)

Gardening

Jardinería

(har – deen – ehr – *ee* – ah)

Go to the cinema

Ir al cine

(eer al see – ne)

Common Questions & Answers
– Preguntas y Respuestas Comúnes

Who is it?

¿Quién es?

(kee – en es)

What is your surname?

¿Cuál es tu apellido?

(kw – *al* es tu ap – eh – ye – doh)

Where did you come from?

¿De dónde viniste?

(de *dohn* – de ven – ees – te)

Where were you born?

¿Dónde naciste?

(*dohn* – de na – sees – te)

I was born in...

Nací en...

(na – *see* en)

How old are you?

¿Cuántos años tienes?

(*kwan* – tos an – *yos* tee – en – es)

I am thirty years old

Tengo treinta años

(ten – go tre – eenta an – *yos*)

Do you have any siblings?

¿Tienes hermanos?

(tee – en – es ehr – mahn – os)

What is your phone number?

¿Cuál es tu numero de teléfono?

(kw – *al* es tu nu – mehr – oh de tel – eh – fo – no)

What is the date today?

¿Cuál es la fecha?

(kw – *al* es la fe – cha)

Do you have pets?

¿Tienes mascotas?

(tee – en –es mahs – ko – tas)

What is the weather like?

¿Qué tiempo hace?

(*ke* tee – em – po ah – se)

It's sunny

Hace sol

(ah – se sol)

It's raining

Está lloviendo

(es – *tah* yo – vee – en – doh)

It's snowing

Está nevando

(es – *tah* neh – vahn – doh)

It's nice out

Hace buen tiempo

(ah – se bwen tee – em – poh)

It's humid

Hace humedad

(ah – se oo – meh – dahd)

It's cloudy

Está nublado

(es – *tah* un – blah – doh)

There's lightning

Hay relámpagos

(ay reh – *lahm* – pah – gos)

There's thunder

Hay truenos

(ay tru – en – ohs)

How much?

¿Cuánto?

(*kwan* - to)

How much is it?

¿Cuánto es?

(*kwan* – to es)

How much does it cost?

¿Cuánto cuesta?

(*kwan* – to kwes – ta)

What do you want?

¿Qué quieres?

(*ke* kee – er – es)

What do you want to do?

¿Qué quieres hacer?

(*ke* kee – er – es ah – ser)

Is it hot? (weather)

¿Hace calor?

(ah – se ka – lor)

Yes, it is hot (weather)

Sí, hace calor

(*see* ah – se ka – lor)

Is it cold? (weather)

¿Hace frio?

(ah – se free – o)

Yes, it is cold (weather)

Sí, hace frio

(*see* ah – se free – o)

Is it hot? (object)

¿Está caliente?

(es – *tah* ka – lee – en – te)

Yes, it is hot (object)

Sí, está caliente

(*see* es – *tah* kal – ee – en –te)

Is it cold? (object)

¿Está frio?

(es – *tah* free – o)

Yes, it is cold (object)

Sí, está frio

(*see* es – *tah* free – o)

How many are there?

¿Cuánto hay?

(*kwan* – toh aye)

Can you repeat that, please?

¿Me lo repite, por favor?

(meh lo reh – pee – te pour - fah – vor)

What is that?

¿Qué es eso?

(*ke* es es – o)

Do you understand?

¿Entiendes?

(en – tee – en – des)

Do you speak English?

¿Hablas inglés?

(ahb – las een – *glehs*)

Yes, I speak English

Sí, hablo inglés

(*see* ahb – lo een – *glehs*)

Where are you going?

¿Adónde vas?

(ah – *dohn* – de vahs)

I'm going over there

Voy por ahı

(voy pour ah – *ye*)

Where is it?

¿Dónde está?

(*dohn* – de es – *tah*)

It's over there

Está por ahí

(es – *tah* pour ah – *ye)*

Why not?

¿Por qué no?

(pour *ke* no)

Why is that?

Y eso. ¿Por qué?

(ee eso pour *ke*)

Whose is that?

¿De quien es eso?

(de ki – en es eso)

It's his

Es suyo

(es soo – yo)

What color is this?

¿Qué color es?

(*ke* koh – lor es)

What is your favorite color?

¿Cuál es tu color favorito?

(*kwal* es tu koh – lor fah – vor – eeto)

Can you help me, please?

¿Puedes ayudarme, por favor?

(pwe – des ah – yu – dar – meh pour fah- vor)

Where is the bathroom?

¿Dónde está el baño?

(*dohn* – de es – *tah* el ban – *yo*)

Is there an ATM around here?

¿Hay un cajero por aquí?

(ay oon ka – hehr – o pour ah – *kee*)

Why? For what purpose?

¿Para qué?

(pa – ra *ke*)

Of what? From what?

¿De qué?

(de *ke*)

Who should I contact?

¿A quién debo contactar?

(ah kee – *en* de – bo kohn – tak – tar)

How do you spell your name?

¿Cómo escribes tu nombre?

(*ko* – mo es – kree – bes tu nohm – bre)

Any questions?

¿Tienes alguna pregunta?

(tee – en – es al – goo – na preh – goon – ta)

Which?

¿Cuál?

(kwal)

Who is he/she?

¿Quién es él/ella?

(kee – *en* es el/eh – ya)

When did you arrive?

¿Cuándo llegaste?

(*kwan* – do yeh – gahs – te)

I arrived last night

Llegue anoche

(yeh – *geh* ah – no – che)

Which is better?

¿Cuál es mejor?

(*kwal* es meh – hor)

This is better

Esto es mejor

(es – toh es meh – hor)

How?

¿Cómo?

(*koh* – mo)

Where did they go?

¿Adonde fueron?

(ah – dohn – de fwer – ohn)

Is he/she here?

¿Él/ella está aquí?

(*el*/eh – ya es – *tah* ah – *kee*)

No, he/she left

No, se fue

(no se fwe)

How many?

¿Cuántos?

(*kwan* – tos)

Why?

¿Por qué?

(pour *ke*)

Because…

Porque…

(pour – ke)

How did you do that?

¿Cómo hiciste eso?

(*koh* – mo ee – sees – te es- oh)

Of course

Claro

(kla – ro)

Of course

Por supuesto

(pour su – pwes – to)

What time do you open?

¿A qué hora abres?

(ah *ke* ora ah – breys)

What time do you close?

¿A qué hora cierres?

(ah *ke* ora see – ehr – res)

How much do I owe you?

¿Cuánto te debo?

(*kwan* – toh te deb – o)

Can I pay with card?

¿Puedo pagar con tarjeta?

(pwe – doh pa – gar kon tar – heh – ta)

Can you deliver it to my hotel?

¿Puedes enviarlo a mi hotel?

(pwe – des ehn – vee –ar – lo ah mee oh – tel)

Reacting to Good News – Reaccionando a Buenas Noticias

Very well

Muy bien

(mooy bee – en)

How nice

Qué bien

(*ke* bee – en)

I'm pleased

Me alegro

(meh ah – le – gro)

I appreciate it

Lo agredezco

(lo ah – gre – des – koh)

Congratulations! (accomplishments)

¡Enhorabuena!

(en – or – ah – bwe – na)

Congratulations! (birthdays, anniversaries, celebrations)

¡Felicidades!

(fe – lee – see – dah – des)

Happy birthday

Feliz Cumpleaños

(fe   leez koom – pley – ahn – yos)

Very well

Muy bien

(mooy bee – en)

It is very good (useful)

Está muy bueno

(es – *tah* mooy bwe – no)

Really?

¿Verdad?

(ver – dahd)

Count me in

Estoy dentro

(es – toy den – tro)

I'm all for it

Me apunto

(meh ah - pun –toh)

Perfect

Perfecto

(pehr – fek – toh)

Stupendous

Estupendo

(es – tu – pen – doh)

Marvelous

Marvilloso

(mar – vee – yo – so)

Absolutely

En absoluto

(en ahb – so – loo – toh)

Awesome

Cojonudo

(ko – ho – nu – doh)

That's it

Eso es

(es – oh es)

That's why

Por eso

(pour es – oh)

Good job

Bien hecho

(bee – en eh – cho)

Magnificent

Magnífico

(mag - neef - ee - koh)

That's how you do it

Eso es cómo se hace

(eso es ko – mo se ah – se)

Brilliant

Genail

(hen – ee – al)

Genius

Genio

(hen – ee – o)

Good idea

Buena idea

(bwe – nah ee – de – ah)

Excellent

Excelente

(ex – sel – len – te)

Incredible

Increible

(een – cre – ee – ble)

Why not?

¿Cómo no?

(ko – mo no)

Ok

De acuerdo

(de ah – kwer – do)

Phenomenal

Fenomenal

(feh – noh – mehn – al)

Funny

Gracioso

(grah – see – oh – so)

Fun

Divertido

(dee – vehr – tee – doh)

I had a good time

Me lo pasé bien

(meh lo pah – *se* bee – en)

What are you doing? - ¿Qué estás haciendo?

What are you doing later?

¿Qué haces luego?

(*ke* ah – cehs loo – eh – go)

What's your plan?

¿Cuál es tu plan?

(*kwal* es tu plahn)

Do you have plans?

¿Qué planes tienes?

(*ke* plahnes tee – en – es)

Do you have planes tonight?

¿Tienes planes esta noche?

(tee – en – es plah – nes es – ta no – che)

Are you going out tonight?

¿Sales esta noche?

(sah – les es – ta no – che)

Clothing & Appearance – Ropa y Aspecto

Handsome (men)

Guapo

(gwa – poh)

Pretty (woman)

Guapa

(gwa – pah)

Pretty

Bonita

(boh – nee – ta)

Beautiful

Hermosa

(ehr – mohs – ah)

Young

Joven

(ho – ven)

Old

Viejo

(vee – ey – ho)

Ugly

Feo

(fe – oh)

Good looking

Buen aspecto

(bwen as – pek – toh)

Smooth

Suave

(swa – veh)

T-shirt

Camiseta

(ka – mee – seta)

Shirt

Camisa

(ka – mee – sa)

Blouse

Blusa

(blu – sa)

Dress

Vestido

(ves – tee – doh)

Bra

Sujetador

(soo – he – tah – dor)

Knickers/Panties

Bragas

(brah – gas)

Tights

Medias

(meh – dee – as)

To dress

Vestirse

(ves – teer – se)

Shoes

Zapatos

(sa – pa – tos)

High heels

Tacones

(ta – kohn – es)

Sneakers/Trainers

Zapatillas

(sa – pa – tee – yas)

Pants/trousers

Pantalones

(pan – tah – loh – nehs)

Jeans

Vaqueros

(va – kehr – os)

Socks

Calcetínes

(kal – se – *tee* – nes)

Underwear

Calzoncillos

(kal – sohn – see – yos)

Shorts

Pantalones cortos

(pan – tah – loh – nehs kor – tos)

Suit

Traje

(tra – hey)

Tie

Corbata

(kor – ba – ta)

Scarf

Bufanda

(boo – fahn – dah)

Ring

Anillo

(ah – nee – yo)

Jewelry

Joyas

(hoy – ahs)

Hat

Gorro

(gor – ro)

Glasses

Gafas

(gah – fas)

Sunglasses

Gafas de sol

(gah – fas de sol)

Sleeves

Mangas

(mahn – gahs)

Size

Talla

(ta – ya)

To dress nice

Vestir arreglado

(ves – teer ahr – reh – glah – doh)

Belt

Cinturon

(sin – tur – ohn)

Button

Botón

(bo – *tohn*)

Bracelet

Pulsera

(pool – ser – ah)

Watch

Reloj

(reh – loh)

Necklace

Collar

(ko – yar)

Earrings

Pendientes

(pen – dee – en – tes)

Dress code

Código de vestimenta

(*ko* – dee go de vehs – tee – mehn – ta)

Dry cleaner's

Tintorería

(teen – toh – rehr – *ee* - ah)

Stain

Mancha

(mahn – cha)

Detergent

Detergente

(de – tehr – hen – te)

To iron

Planchar

(plahn – char)

Short

Corto

(kor – toh)

Long

Largo

(lahr – go)

Straight (hair)

Liso

(lee – so)

Curly

Rizado

(ree – sah – doh)

Blond

Rubio

(ru – bee – oh)

Red-head

Pelirrojo

(pel – eer – roh – ho)

Light brown

Castaño

(kahs – tan – *yo*)

Dark brown

Moreno

(moh – rey – no)

Black

Negro

(neh – gro)

Gray

Canoso

(kahn – oso)

Tall

Alto

(ahl – toh)

Short

Bajo

(bah – ho)

Medium

Mediano

(med – ee – ano)

Fat

Gordo

(gor – doh)

Thin

Flaco

(flah – ko)

Red

Rojo

(ro – ho)

Blue

Azul

(ah – sul)

Green

Verde

(vehr – de)

Light

Claro

(klah – ro)

Dark

Oscuro

(ohs – ku – ro)

What do you look like?

¿Cómo te ves?

(*ko* – mo te ves)

Problem Solving – Resolver Problemas

Problem

Problema

(pro – bleh – ma)

To solve

Resolver

(reh – sol – vehr)

Solution

Solución

(soh – lu – see – *ohn*)

Mess

Lío

(*lee* – oh)

Big problem

Gran problema

(grahn pro – bleh – ma)

Let's try this

Hacemos una cosa

(ah – semos oona ko – sa)

To try

Probar

(pro – bar)

Intend

Intentar

(een – ten – tar)

Issue

Asunto

(ah – soon – toh)

Matter

Tema

(te – ma)

Solve the matter

Cerrar el tema

(ser – rar el te – ma)

What's the problem?

¿Qué es el problema?

(*ke* es el pro – bleh – ma)

What's the matter with you?

¿Qué te pasa?

(*ke* te pah – sa)

Don't get annoyed

No te enfades

(no te ehn – fah – des)

Cheer up

Ánimo

(*ah* – nee – mo)

The Body – El cuerpo

Head

Cabeza

(kah – bey – sah)

Neck

Cuello

(kwey – yo)

Shoulders

Hombros

(ohm – bros)

Chest

Pecho

(peh – cho)

Arms

Brazos

(brah – sohs)

Waist

Lintura

(sin – too – rah)

Hips

Cadera

(kah – dehr – ah)

Wrist

Muñeca

(moon – *yeh* – ka)

Hands

Manos

(mah – nos)

Fingers

Dedos

(deh – dohs)

Nails

Uñas

(oon – *yas*)

Legs

Piernas

(pee – ehr – nahs)

Ankle

Tobillo

(toh – bee – yo)

Heel

Talón

(tah – *lohn*)

Feet

Pies

(pee – eys)

Toes

Dedos de pie

(deh – dohs de pee- ey)

Knee

Rodilla

(ro – dee – ya)

Elbow

Codo

(ko – doh)

Buttocks

Nalgas

(nahl – ga)

Hair

Pelo

(peh – lo)

Eyes

Ojos

(oh – hos)

Nose

Nariz

(nar – ees)

Ear

Oreja

(oh – rey – ha)

Lips

Labios

(lah – bee – ohs)

Cheek

Mejilla

(meh – hee – ya)

Mustache

Bigote

(bee – go – te)

You're growing a mustache

Dejaste el bigote

(de – hahs – te el bee – go – te)

Beard

Barba

(bar – ba)

To shave

Afietarse

(ah – feh – tar – se)

To wax

Depilarse

(deh – pee – lahr – se)

Bikini line

Las ingles

(lahs een – glehs)

Underarms

Axilas

(ah   see – las)

Bone

Hueso

(weys – oh)

Joint

Articulación

(ahr – tee – coo – lah – see – on)

Break

Romper

(rohm – pehr)

Break a bone

Romper el hueso

(rohm – pehr el weys – oh)

Have a headache

Tener un dolor de cabeza

(te – ner oon do – lor de cah – beh – sa)

Toothache

Dolor de muelas

(do – lor deh moo – eh – las)

Pull a muscle

Tensarse el músculo

Haircut

Cortar el pelo

(kor – tar el peh – lo)

Style your hair

Peinar el pelo

(pey – ee – nar el peh – lo)

Airplanes & Airports – Aviónes y Aeropuertos

How long does it take to get to the airport?

¿Cuánto tarda a llegar al aeropuerto?

(kwan – toh tahr – da ah yeh – gar al ehr –o – pwer – toh)

Gate

Puerta

(pwer – tah)

Flight

Vuelo

(vweh – lo)

Passengers

Pasajeros

(pah – sah – hehr – ohs)

Luggage

Equipaje

(eh – kee – pah – hey)

Bags

Maletas

(mah – leh – tas)

Ticket

Billete

(bee – ye – te)

Boarding pass

Tarjeta de embarque

(tar – heh – ta de ehm – bar – ke)

Pilot

Piloto

(pee – loh – toh)

Emergency exit

Salida de emergencia

(sah – lee – da de eh – mehr – hen – see – ah)

Seat

Asiento

(ah – see – en – toh)

Row

Fila

(fee – la)

Flight attendant

Azafata

(ahs – ah – fa – ta)

Carry-on luggage

Equipaje de mano

(eh – kee – pah – hey de mah – no)

Arrival

Llegada

(Ye – gah – dah)

What time do you arrive?

¿A qué hora llegas?

(ah *ke* ora ye – gahs)

I arrive at 9:30 p.m.

Llego a las nueve y media de la noche

(ye – go ah lahs nu – eh – ve de la no – che)

Departure

Salida

(sah – lee – da)

Take-off

El despegue

(el des – peh – geh)

Landing

El aterrizaje

(el ah – tehr – ree – sah – hey)

Delay

Retraso

(reh – tras – o)

Why has the plane been delayed?

¿Por qué el avión está retrasado?

(pour *ke* el ahv – *ee* – ohn es – *ta* reh – tras – ah – doh)

My seatbelt won't fasten

Mi cinturón no abrocha

(mee seen – tur – *ohn* no ah – bro – cha)

May I have a blanket?

¿Puedo tener una manta?

(pwe – doh teh – nehr oona mahn – ta)

I'd like a vegetarian meal

Quisiera una comida vegetariana

(kees – ee – ehra oona ko – mee – da veh – heh – tar – ee – ahna)

What time are we going to land?

¿A qué hora vamos a aterrizar?

(ah *ke* ohra vah – mos ah ah – tehr – ree – sar)

Can I change my seat?

¿Puedo cambiar mi asiento?

(pwe – doh kam – bee – ar mee ah – see – en – toh)

I'd like an aisle seat

Quisiera un asiento junto al pasillo

(kees – ee – ehra oon ah – see – en – toh hun – toh ahl pa – see – yo)

I'd like a window seat

Quisiera un asiento junto a la ventana

(kees – ee – ehra oon ah – see – en – toh hun – toh ah la vehn – tahn – ah)

What is the in-flight movie?

¿Cuál es la pelicula del vuelo?

(*kwal* es la peh – lee – ku – la del vu – eh – lo)

May I have some water?

¿Puedo tener agua por favor?

(pwe – doh teh – nehr ah – gwa pour fah – vor)

Sentence Starters – Empezar una frase

Do you have a sec?
¿Me prestas un segundo?
(meh preh – stas oon seh – goon – doh)

Wow!
¡Ala!
(ah – lah)

Damn!
¡Jolín!
(ho – *leen*)

Well, so what?
¿Bueno, y que?
(bweh – no, ee ke)

Well then...
Bueno...
(bweh – no)

And you know what else?
¿Y sabes que más?
(ee sah – bez ke *mahz*)

On second thought, (I do want a beer!)
Pensándolo bien, (¡sí quiero una cerveza!)
(pehn – *san* – do – lo bee – en, *see* kee – eh –ro oo – na ser – ver – sa)

What a relief!
¡Qué alivio!
(*ke* ah – lee – vee – o)

Well...
Pues...
(pweh – z)

You'd better do it, because otherwise...
Más vale que lo hagas, porque si no...
(*mah* – z bah – leh ke lo ah – gas, por – ke see no)

I'd love to help you but...
Me encantaría ayudarte/os pero...
(meh ehn – cahn – tah – *ree* – ya ah – yoo – dahr – te/ os peh – ro)

Oops!
¡Uy!
(oo – ee)

Let's see...
A ver...
(ah ver)

Ok, but...
Vale, pero...
(bah – le, peh – ro)

Trust me
Confía en mí
(cohn – *fee* – ya en *mee*)

Come on!
¡Anda!
(ahn – dah)

Maybe so, but...
Tal vez, pero...
(tahl bes, peh – ro)

Hey!
¡Oye!
(o – yeh)

Look out
Cuidado
(kwee – dah – do)

On the contrary...
Al contrario...
(ahl con – trah – ree – o)

You don't say
No me digas
(no meh dee – gaz)

Excuse me...
Perdón...
(pehr – *don*)

Sorry, but...

Lo siento, pero...

(lo see – ehn – to, peh – ro)

Do you know of a restaurant around here?

¿Conoces algún (restaurante por aqui)?

(co no sez al goon rez – tau – rahn – te por ah – kee)

Shopping & Negotiating – Comprando y Negociando

Where are the shops?
¿Dónde están las tiendas?
(*don* - deh ehs - *tanh* lahz tee – en – daz)

I don't need any help, I'm just browsing, thanks
No necesito ayuda, sólo estoy ojeando, gracias
(no neh – seh – see – to ah – yu – dah, *so* – lo ehs – toi o – heh – an – do,
grah – see – az)

Is this on sale?
¿Esto está rebajado?
(ehs - to esh - *tah* reh - bah - jah - do)

I'm looking for a pair of jeans
Busco unos vaqueros
(boo-sko oo-nos bah-ke-ros)

Do you have these jeans in a size 40?
¿Tienes estos vaqueros en la talla cuarenta?
(tee - eh - nez ehs - tos ba - ke - ros ehn la tai - ya kwa - rehn – tah)

Do you have them in stock?
¿Los tenéis en stock?
(loz teh - *neiz* en stock)

Where are the fitting rooms?
¿Dónde están los probadores?
(*don* - deh ehs - *tan* los pro - bah - do - rez)

Try it on
Probarlo
(p – ro - bah - lo)

Where is the till?
¿Dónde está la caja?
(*don* - deh ehs - *tah* lah kah - ha?)

How much is it?
¿Cuanto vale?
(kwan-to bah-lei)

Is this returnable?
¿Esto se puede devolver?
(ehs - to seh poo - eh - deh deh - vol - ver)

This ítem is damaged, can I get a discount?
¿Este producto está defectuoso, me podéis hacer un descuento?
(ehs - teh pro - dook - to eh - *stah* deh - fehk - too - o - so, meh po - *dei* - z ah - ser oon dehz - kwen - to)

Do you do student discount?
¿Hacéis descuento de estudiante?
(ah - *seiz* dehz - kwen - to deh ehs - too - dee - an - teh)

Do you take card?

¿Aceptáis tarjeta?

(ah - seh - p - *taiz* tahr - heh - tah)

Keep the change

Quédate el cambio

(keh - dah - teh el kam - bee - o)

May I have the receipt?

¿Me puede dar el ticket de compra?

(meh pweh – deh dahr el tee – ket deh com – prah)

You've charged me twice for this

Me has cobrado dos veces por esto

(meh ahz co - brah - do doz veh - sehs poor ehz - to)

This item is damaged, I want to return it.

Este producto está defectuoso, quiero devolverlo.

(ehs - teh pro - dook - to eh - *stah* deh - fehk - too - o- so, key - eh - roh deh
- vol - ver
- lo.)

I want to return this.

Quiero hacer una devolución.

(key-eh-ro ah - ser oo-nah deh – voh - loo- see -on)

I want to exchange this.

Quiero cambiar esto.

(kee - eh - ro kam - bee - ahr ehs - to)

Where is the supermarket?

Dónde está el supermercado?

(*don* - deh ehs - *tah* el su - pehr - mehr - kah - do?)

What aisle is the fresh produce in?

En que pasillo están los productos frescos?

(ehn ke pah - see - yo ehs - *tahn* loz pro - dook - tos frehz - koz?)

Where is the check out counter?

Dónde está la caja?

(*don* - deh ehs - *tah* lah kah - ha?)

Are you open on Sundays?

Abren los domingos?

(ah – bren los do – min – gos?)

Can you give me a cost estimate?

Me puedes dar una estimación del coste?

(meh pweh - dehz dahr oo - nah ehz - tee - mah - see – *on* del kohs - te)

That's too much

No vale tanto.

(no ba - leh tahn - to)

Take it or leave it.

Tómalo o déjalo.

(*to* – mah - lo o *deh* - ha - lo)

I'll give you five euros

Te doy cinco euros

(teh doi seen - ko ew - ros)

I'll give you eight euros for these two

Te doy ocho euros por estos dos

(teh doi oh - tcho euh - ros por ehs - toz doz)

It's a real bargain

Es una auténtica ganga

(ehz oo - nah ow - *ten* - tee - kah gan - ha)

What a rip off

Vaya timo

(ba – ya tee – mo)

Dating & Personal – Relaciónes y Personal

To flirt

Ligar

(lee – gar)

Do you have a lighter?
¿Tienes fuego?
(tee – eh – nez fweh – go?)

Do you have a cigarette?

¿Tienes un cigarro?

(tee – ehn – ehs oon see – gahr – roh)

I don't smoke
No fumo
(no foo – mo)

You're pretty
Eres guapa
(eh - rez gwa - pa)

You're beautiful
Qué bonita eres
(keh boh – nee - ta ehr - es)

That's so cheesy!
¡Qué cursi!
(*keh* coor-see)

I find you interesting
Me atraes
(meh ah – traiz)

Would you like to go out with me?
¿Quieres salir conmigo?
(kee – eh – rez sah – lee – r con – mee – go)

I'll pick you up at 8
Te recojo a las ocho
(teh reh – co – ho ah laz o – tcho)

I've reserved a table.
He reservado una mesa
(eh reh – ser – ba – do oo – nah meh – sa)

This rounds on me.
Yo pago esta ronda
(yo pah – go ehs – tah ron – dah)

Let me buy you a drink.
Te invito a una copa.
(teh een – vee – to ah oo – nah co – pah)

Can I buy you a drink?
¿Te puedo invitar a una copa?
(teh pweh – do een – vee – tahr ah oo – nah co – pah)

May I join you?
¿Te puedo acompañar?
(teh pweh – do ah – com – pah – yiar)

Are you from around here?
¿Eres de aquí?
(eh – rez deh ah – kee)

I'm from London.
Soy de Londres.
(soi deh lon – drez.)

What do you do?
En que trabajas?
(ehn ke trah – bah – haz?)

I'm a teacher.
Soy profesor/a.
(soi pro – feh – sor/so – rah.)

Did you study at university?
¿Has estudiado en la universidad?
(ahz ehs – too – dee – ah – do en lah oo – nee – ber – see – dad)

I studied French

Estudie francés

(ehs – too – dee – eh frahn – *sez*)

What are you studying?

¿Qué estudias?

(ke ehz – too – dee – az)

I'm studying architecture

Estudio arquitectura

(ehz – too – di – o ahr – kee – tec – too – rah)

Do you have a boyfriend?

¿Tienes novio?

(tee – ehn – es no – vee – o)

Do you have a girlfriend?

¿Tienes novia?

(tee – ehn – es no – vee – ah)

To be engaged

Estar comprometido

(es – star kom – pro – meh – tee – doh)

Are you married?

¿Estás casado?

(ehs – *tahs* kah – sah – do)

Yes, I'm married.

Sí, estoy casado

(*see*, ehs – toi cah – sah – do)

I'm single

Estoy soltero

(ehs – toi sol – teh – rah)

Do you have kids?

Tienes hijos?

(tee – eh – nez ee – hoz)

Yes, I have two kids

Sí, tengo dos niños

(*see*, tehn – go dos nee – *yoz*)

Do you have any siblings?

¿Tienes hermanos?

(tee – eh – nez ehr – mah – noz)

Yes, I have a brother and a sister

Sí, tengo un hermano y una hermana

(*see*, tehn – go oon ehr – mah – no ee oo-na ehr – mah – nah)

I'm an only child

Soy hijo único

(soi ee – ho *oo* – nee – co)

Do you like dancing?

¿Te gusta bailar?

(teh goo – stah bai – lahr)

I like dancing salsa

Me gusta bailar sals.

(meh goo – stah bai – lar salsa)

Do you like Spanish food?

¿Te gusta la comida española?

(teh goo – stah la co – mee – dah ez – pah – *yo* – la)

I love Portuguese food

Me encanta la comida portuguesa

(meh en – kan – tah lah ko – mee – dah por – too – geh – sa.)

What music do you like?

¿Qué música te gusta?

(ke *moo* – zee – ca teh goo – stah)

I like hip hop

Me gusta el hip hop

(meh goo – stah el hip hop)

Do you like travelling?

¿Te gusta viajar?

(teh goo – stah bee – ah – har)

Where have you travelled to?
¿Qué has visitado?
(*ke* ahz bee – zee – tah – do)

Have you been to Barcelona?

¿Conoces a Barcelona?

(ko – no – sehs ah bar – seh – lo – nah)

I love being with you
Estoy a gusto a tu lado
(ehs – toi ah goos – to ah too lah – do)

It's been a delightful evening
Ha sido una velada encantadora
(ah see – do oo – nah no – che en – can – tah – do – rah)

I had a wonderful time
Lo he pasado en grande
(lo eh pah – sah – do en grahn – deh)

Do you live nearby?
¿Vives por aquí cerca?
(vee – behz por ah – kee ser – ka)

I live in the centre
Vivo por el centro
(bee – bo por el sen – tro)

I live nearby
Vivo cerca de aquí
(bee – bo deh ah – kee)

I live far away
Vivo lejos
(bee – bo leh – hoz)

Shall we split the bill?

Compartimos la cuenta?
(com – pahr – tee – moz la kwen – tah?)

Shall we go dutch?
Vamos a medias?
(vah – moz ah meh – dee – az?)

My treat!
Invito yo!
(een – bee – to yo!)

Shall I drop you off at home?

¿Te acero a casa?

(teh ah – ser – co ah cah – sah?)

Let me walk you home

Te acompaño a casa

(tch ah   com – pah – yo ah cah – sah)

Do you want to come back to mine?

¿Quieres venir a mi casa?

(kee – eh – rez veh – neer ah mee cah – sa)

I can't take my eyes off you

No puedo dejar de mirarte

(no pweh – do deh – har de mee – rah – te)

You turn me on

Me pones muy cachondo

(meh po – nez moo – ee cah – con – do)

Do you have a condom?

¿Tienes un condon?

(tee – eh – nez oon con – don)

To date/go out with someone

Salir con alguien

(sah – leer kon al – gi – en)

To cheat

Ponerse cuernos

(po – nehr – se kwer – nos)

Third Wheel

Sujeta velas

(soo – he – tah be – las)

To make out

Morrear

(mo – reh – ar)

One-night stand

Un polvo

(oon pol – vo)

To have a one-night stand

Echar un polvo

(eh – char oon pol – vo)

To be in a relationship with someone

Estar en una relación con alguien

(es – tar en oona reh – la – see – *ohn* kon al – gi – en)

Conclusion – Conclusión

There you have it! Hopefully now you are prepared to take on your adventure in the Spanish language. Remember to be careful with the masculine and feminine forms, practice your pronunciation, and conjugate your verbs correctly. Now go out catch a bullfight, sail around the Caribbean, or simply impress the wait staff at you favorite Mexican restaurant. ¡Hasta luego!

Made in the USA
Middletown, DE
18 September 2016